Paper Crafts for Halloween

Randel McGee

Enslow Elementary

an imprint of

Enslow Publishers, Inc.

40 Industrial Road
Box 398
Berkeley Heights, NJ 07922
USA

http://www.enslow.com

To my sons, Nathan, Adam, Matthew, and Aaron
for always making Halloween a fun time with their
homemade costumes and funny tricks.

A special thank you to Karol Krěmár for his inspiring paper crafts.

Copyright © 2009 by Randel McGee.

This book meets the National Standards for Arts Education standards.

Enslow Elementary, an imprint of Enslow Publishers, Inc.
Enslow Elementary® is a registered trademark of Enslow Publishers, Inc.

Library of Congress Cataloging-in-Publication Data

McGee, Randel.
    Paper crafts for Halloween / Randel McGee.
        p. cm. — (Paper craft fun for holidays)
    Summary: "Provides a brief introduction to the history of Halloween, and Halloween-themed paper craft
        ideas"—Provided by publisher.
    Includes bibliographical references and index.
    ISBN-13: 978-0-7660-2947-7
    ISBN-10: 0-7660-2947-6
    1. Halloween decorations—Juvenile literature. 2. Paper work—Juvenile literature. I. Title.
    TT900.H32M367 2009
    745.594'1646—dc22   2007014048

Printed in the United States of America

10 9 8 7 6 5 4 3 2 1

To Our Readers:
We have done our best to make sure all Internet addresses in this book were active and appropriate when we went to press. However, the author and the publisher have no control over and assume no liability for the material available on those Internet sites or on other Web sites they may link to. Any comments or suggestions can be sent by e-mail to comments@enslow.com or to the address on the back cover.

Every effort has been made to locate all copyright holders of material used in this book. If any errors or omissions have occurred, corrections will be made in future editions of this book.

♻ Enslow Publishers, Inc., is committed to printing our books on recycled paper. The paper in every book contains 10% to 30% post-consumer waste (PCW). The cover board on the outside of each book contains 100% PCW. Our goal is to do our part to help young people and the environment too!

Illustration Credits: Crafts prepared by Randel McGee; Photography by Nicole diMella/Enslow Publishers, Inc.; Shutterstock, p. 5; Courtesy of Jane Katirgis/Enslow Publishers, Inc., pp. 33 (foreground), 37 (both).

Cover Illustration: Crafts prepared by Randel McGee; Photography by Nicole diMella/Enslow Publishers, Inc.

CONTENTS

Halloween! 4

1. Scarecrow Jumping Jack 6

2. Flying Bat 11

3. Haunted House With Ghosts 15

4. Bat and Ghost Chains 20

5. Standing Little Witchie 24

6. Sitting Black Cat 28

7. Skull Headdress 31

8. Goofy Goggles 34

Patterns 38

Read About
(Books and Internet Addresses) 45

Index 46

About the Author 47

Halloween!

What a night! An evening of mystery and mischief, masks and make-believe, fun and fantasies! A holiday that is centuries old, yet always seems to keep up with the times! What night is this? Why, All Hallows' Even or Halloween!

This holiday had its beginning in ancient times. The Celts were people that lived in northern Europe, England, Scotland, and Ireland thousands of years ago. They celebrated the end of the summer, the end of their year, and the harvest season on a day that we know as October 31. They called the day Samhain (SOW-in). It was thought that on this night the spirits of the dead could return to earth. These spirits could do mischief and harm to the living, so people disguised themselves as spirits or scary creatures to fool them.

Druids were the spiritual leaders of the Celts and were thought to have special powers to understand the forces of nature. On this night the druids would light a big bonfire. People from miles around would put out their home fires and then travel to the bonfire to collect hot embers. The embers were used to relight their fires as a sign of a new beginning to the year.

Roman armies conquered the Celts by A.D. 43. The Romans had their own holidays for honoring the dead and celebrating the harvest. The Celts accepted many of the Roman celebrations and mixed them with their own traditions. Christianity came to the Celts and brought with it many of its holidays.

During the 800s, the Catholic pope, Boniface IV, declared November 1 as All Hallows' Mass. *Hallow* meant "a saint" or "holy person," so this was a day

to honor all the saints. The evening before this day became known as All Hallows' Even, and over the years, was shortened to Halloween.

November 2 was All Souls' Day, the day to honor all loved ones who had died. On this day, English children would go "a souling," visiting neighbors for little "soul cakes," treats made to reward the children for saying prayers for the dead. This may be where the tradition of trick-or-treating started.

November 2 is still celebrated in many Spanish-speaking countries as the Day of the Dead, or Día de los Muertos. These two days and the night before them were known as Hallowmas.

Halloween was a popular holiday in old Ireland. It is from the Irish that we get the traditions of wearing costumes and carving jack-o'-lanterns for Halloween. Thousands of Irish came to the United States during the 1800s. They brought with them their Halloween traditions. Halloween became a popular holiday for Americans. It is a day of fun, dressing up in costumes, and community sharing.

5

SCARECROW JUMPING JACK

The scarecrow is used to scare away unwanted pests from gardens and fields. It is a protector of the fruits and vegetables that are part of the harvest. The scarecrow makes a great symbol of Halloween because he scares away pesky animals, has a funny face, and is usually dressed in old clothes. This scarecrow can also jump and dance, which is sure to scare away any pest that comes his way.

WHAT YOU WILL NEED

- tracing paper
- pencil
- white glue
- light cardboard
- crayons or markers
- scissors

- hole punch
- ruler
- string
- paper fasteners
- bead (plastic or wood), about the size of a large pea

WHAT TO DO:

A)

1. Use tracing paper to transfer the pattern of the scarecrow and all the parts from page 40.

2. Glue the tracing paper with the pattern onto light cardboard (See A).

B)

3. Decorate the scarecrow and the different parts as you wish with markers or crayons.

4. Cut the pattern out of the light cardboard (See B).

7

9. Hang on to the string at the top of the scarecrow and gently tug on the bead to make the scarecrow's arms and legs swing and jump.

FLYING BAT

The bat has long been a symbol of Halloween—but why? The ancient Celts built huge bonfires on the night that they thought the dead returned to earth. These bright fires probably attracted thousands of moths, mosquitoes, and flies, and these insects are bats' favorite foods. People would see the bats swooping above the fire. They thought the bats were the pets of witches and evil spirits. We now know that bats are harmless, helpful animals, and not evil. Here is a bat to swoop over your Halloween party.

WHAT YOU WILL NEED

- tracing paper
- pencil
- brown or black construction paper
- scissors
- crayons or markers
- colored chalk (optional)
- string
- ruler
- clear tape

WHAT TO DO:

1. Use tracing paper to transfer the pattern from page 41 to dark construction paper.

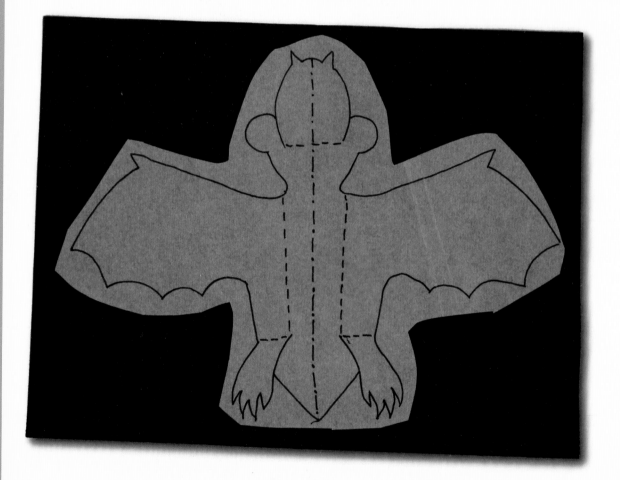

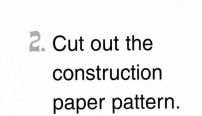

2. Cut out the construction paper pattern.

3. Fold the figure along the fold lines of the pattern.

4. Decorate the bat figure with markers, crayons, or colored chalk.

5. Tape a 12- to 14-inch-long string in the middle of the back between the wings.

6. **Ask an adult** to hang the bat from the ceiling or window frame.

HAUNTED HOUSE WITH GHOSTS

Have you ever seen an empty old house that is slowly falling apart? It seems there is nothing inside but the memories of those who lived there long ago. It could be the perfect place for a ghost or two to hide away from the hustle and bustle of the living world. Since ancient times, people have always felt a connection between empty houses or ruins and the spirits of those who once lived there. Here is a haunted house with some friendly ghosts.

WHAT YOU WILL NEED

- tracing paper
- pencil
- construction paper in any color—12 inches x 18 inches
- scissors
- ruler
- white office paper
- markers or crayons
- colored pencils (optional)
- clear tape
- white paper towel (optional)

15

WHAT TO DO:

A)

1. Use tracing paper to transfer the house pattern on page 39 on a sheet of construction paper folded widthwise.

2. Cut out the house pattern along the solid lines. Cut out the windows (See A).

3. Cut a 7-inch by 5½-inch rectangle from a different colored construction paper for the roof (See B).

B)

4. Draw four or five ghosts on white office paper. See page 38 for the pattern. Cut them out (See C).

C)

16

5. Use markers, crayons, or colored pencils to decorate the house with doors, window frames, shutters, or other features. Use markers or crayons to decorate the roof.

6. Fold the house pattern along the fold lines of the pattern to form the four corners of the house. One side will be open where the two edges meet. Fold the roof piece in half widthwise.

7. Tape some ghosts to the inside of four or five windows. If you wish, make curtains by tearing off a small piece of white paper towel. Tape the small piece inside a window.

8. Tape the open side of the house closed. Tape the roof on top. Tape the whole house onto a sheet of construction paper.

BAT AND GHOST CHAINS

What do bats and ghosts have in common? They both live in abandoned buildings and ruins, they both come out at night, they both can fly, and they are both symbols of Halloween. Bats and ghosts will hover above your party when you make this paper chain to decorate your walls and ceiling.

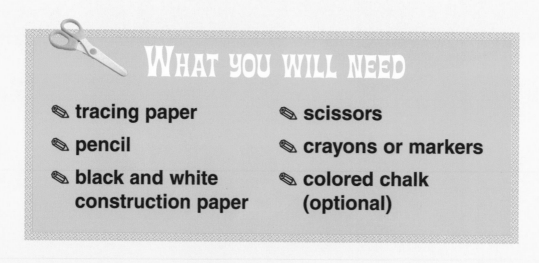

WHAT YOU WILL NEED

- tracing paper
- pencil
- black and white construction paper
- scissors
- crayons or markers
- colored chalk (optional)

WHAT TO DO:

1. Use tracing paper to transfer the bat pattern from page 41 to black construction paper. Use tracing paper to transfer the ghost pattern from page 41 to white construction paper.

2. Cut out at least six pieces of each pattern. Be sure to cut out the center of the ovals on each side of the patterns as indicated.

3. Decorate the bats and ghosts as you wish with markers, crayons, or colored chalk.

4. Link the pieces together by gently folding the oval on one side of a figure and inserting it into the oval of another figure.

5. Gently unfold the oval you just inserted so that it will not slip back out through the hole.

6. Repeat steps 4 and 5 until you have a long chain of paper bats and ghosts. **Ask an adult** to hang the chain along the wall or ceiling to decorate a room.

STANDING LITTLE WITCHIE

A witch was once thought to be a wise woman with a special knowledge of helpful plants. Over the centuries, stories about witches often gave them magical and evil powers. Stories would say that witches would gather together on Halloween and celebrate by a bonfire. They wore black clothes and pointed black hats, and they had black cats as pets. They would dance with brooms and pretend to ride them. Witches are still a popular part of Halloween decorations and costumes. Here is a friendly little witch to celebrate Halloween with you.

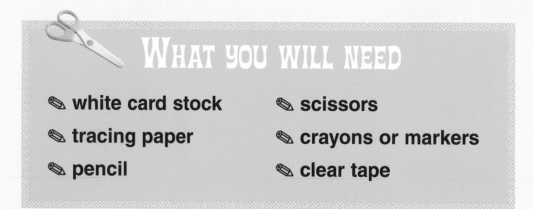

WHAT YOU WILL NEED

- white card stock
- tracing paper
- pencil
- scissors
- crayons or markers
- clear tape

What to do:

1. Fold the white card stock in half lengthwise.

2. Use tracing paper to transfer the pattern from page 42 to white card stock (See A). Place the straight edge of the pattern along the fold of the card stock.

A)

B)

3. Cut out the pattern along the black lines (See B).

4. Decorate the figure as you wish with crayons or markers (See C).

C)

D)

5. Fold the arms slightly forward. Fold the nose slightly forward and pinch it gently (See D).

6. Tape the sides of the skirt together behind the figure.

26

7. Stand the figure up on a table or desk to watch over your Halloween celebration.

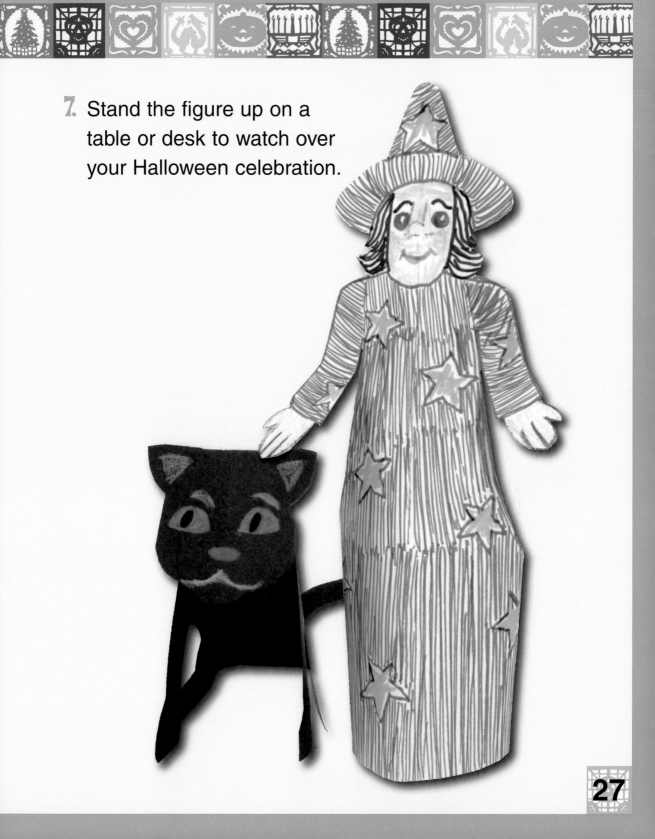

SITTING BLACK CAT

Black is the color most often associated with death and the unknown. Cats are sly and slinky creatures that move around easily in the black of night. Superstitious people throughout the ages believed that black cats were unlucky, strange, or wicked; the favorite pets of witches. Here is a tame black cat that only wants to watch how you celebrate Halloween.

WHAT YOU WILL NEED

- ✎ tracing paper
- ✎ pencil
- ✎ black construction paper
- ✎ scissors
- ✎ colored chalk
- ✎ colored pencils (optional)

WHAT TO DO:

1. Use tracing paper to transfer the pattern from page 43 to black construction paper.

2. Cut out the pattern.

3. Decorate the cat figure with colored chalk or colored pencils.

4. Fold the figure along the dotted lines of the pattern.

5. Set the cat up as a decoration on your table or in your room.

30

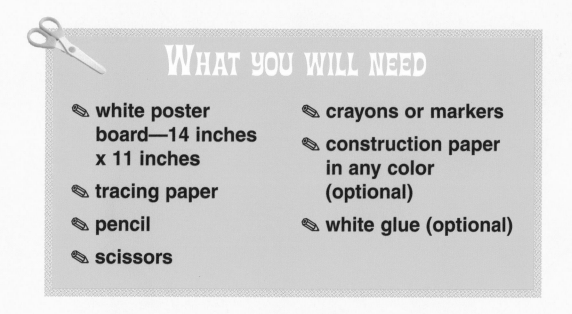

SKULL HEADDRESS

Skulls and skeletons represent the dead. Halloween is the night when spirits of the dead were thought to roam the earth. People long ago would disguise themselves with hoods and masks to fool the dead and avoid being bothered or tricked by mischievous ghosts. This quick and easy skull headdress might not trick your living friends, but it can still add some fun to Halloween.

WHAT YOU WILL NEED

- white poster board—14 inches x 11 inches
- tracing paper
- pencil
- scissors
- crayons or markers
- construction paper in any color (optional)
- white glue (optional)

WHAT TO DO:

1. Fold the poster board in half widthwise so that the shorter sides meet.

2. Use tracing paper to transfer the pattern from page 44 to the poster board.

3. Cut out the poster board pattern. Cut along all the solid lines.

4. Open the folded poster board and decorate the skull headdress as you wish with crayons or markers. If you wish, use construction paper to make eyes. Glue them on the headdress. Let dry.

5. Gently push back the bottom jaw of the skull and slip it carefully over your head.

Goofy Goggles

Halloween has always been a day of costumes and masks, disguises and funny faces. At the beginning of the twentieth century in America, Halloween became a more community-centered event with neighborhood parties or trick-or-treating, visiting neighbors' homes to receive a little treat. When I was a child, half the fun of Halloween was putting together my own costumes and disguises to show my friends. Making my own costumes and decorations was fun and creative. In America today it is estimated that almost $7 billion are spent for Halloween!

What you will need

- poster board in any color—4 inches x 7 inches
- ruler
- tracing paper
- pencil
- scissors
- crayons or markers
- construction paper in any color (optional)
- craft feathers (optional)
- glitter (optional)
- white glue (optional)

34

WHAT TO DO:

1. Fold the poster board in half widthwise, so that the short sides meet.

2. Use tracing paper to transfer the goggle pattern from page 44 to the poster board.

3. Cut out the pattern. Be sure to cut out the holes for the eyes as shown on the pattern.

4. Lay the goggles out flat and decorate them as you wish using crayons, markers, construction paper, craft feathers, glitter, and glue. Let dry.

5. Gently push back the top part of the goggles and slip it over your head.

PATTERNS

Use tracing paper to copy the patterns on these pages.
Ask an adult to help you cut and trace the shapes.

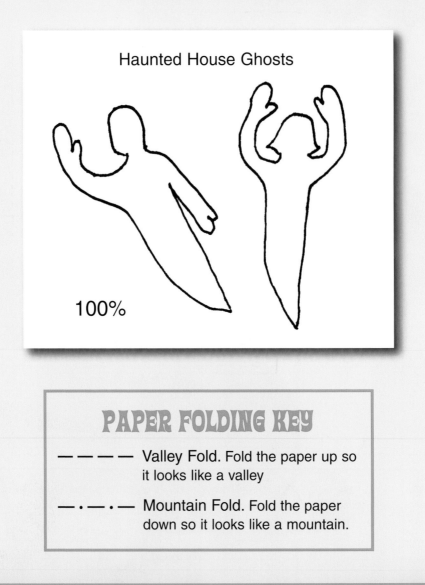

Haunted House Ghosts

100%

PAPER FOLDING KEY

— — — — Valley Fold. Fold the paper up so it looks like a valley

— · — · — Mountain Fold. Fold the paper down so it looks like a mountain.

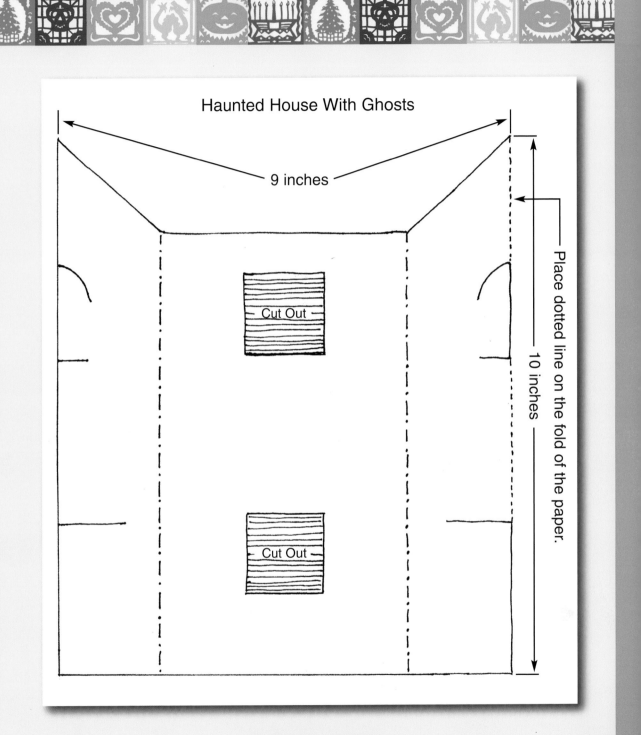

Haunted House With Ghosts

9 inches

Cut Out

Cut Out

Place dotted line on the fold of the paper.

10 inches

Enlarge 125%

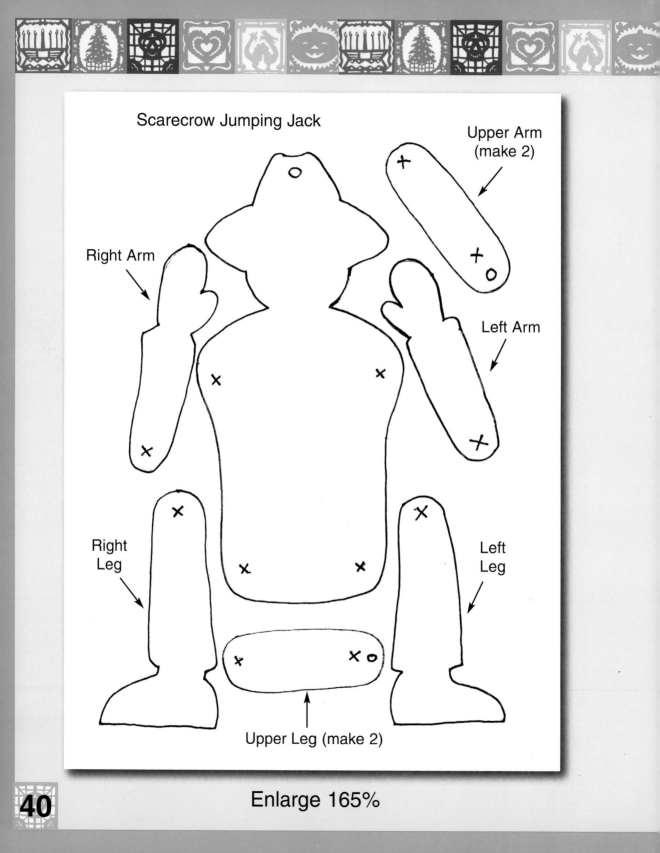

Scarecrow Jumping Jack

Upper Arm
(make 2)

Right Arm

Left Arm

Right
Leg

Left
Leg

Upper Leg (make 2)

Enlarge 165%

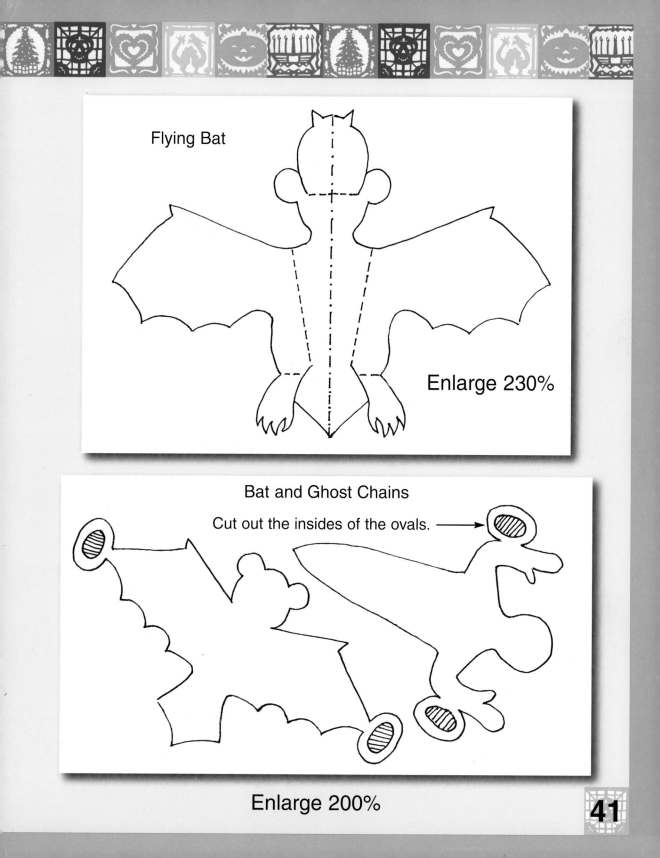

Flying Bat

Enlarge 230%

Bat and Ghost Chains

Cut out the insides of the ovals.

Enlarge 200%

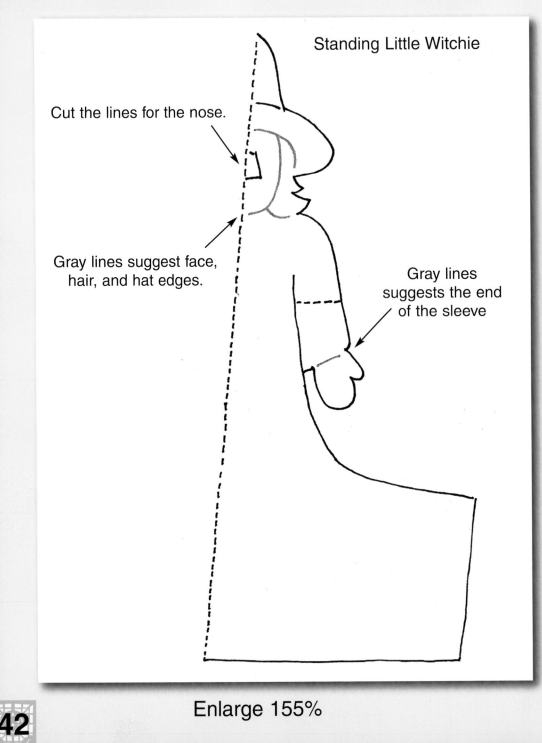

Standing Little Witchie

Cut the lines for the nose.

Gray lines suggest face,
hair, and hat edges.

Gray lines
suggests the end
of the sleeve

42

Enlarge 155%

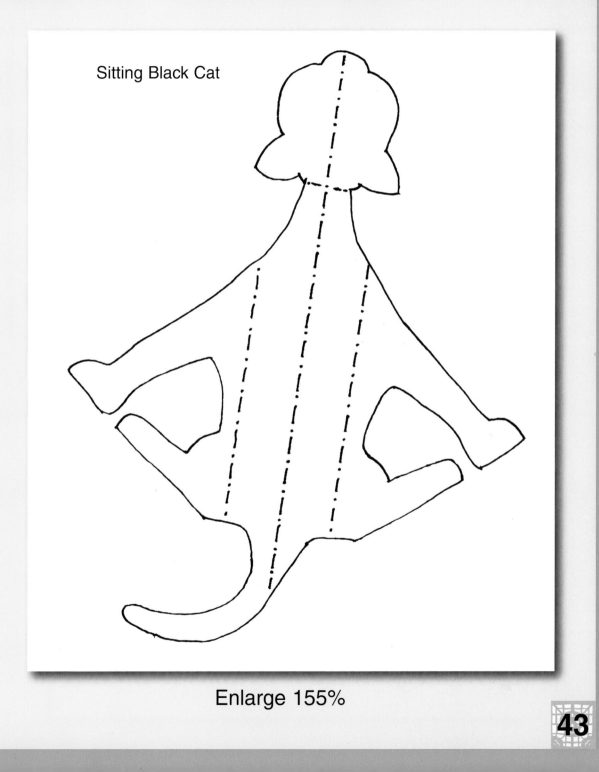

Sitting Black Cat

Enlarge 155%

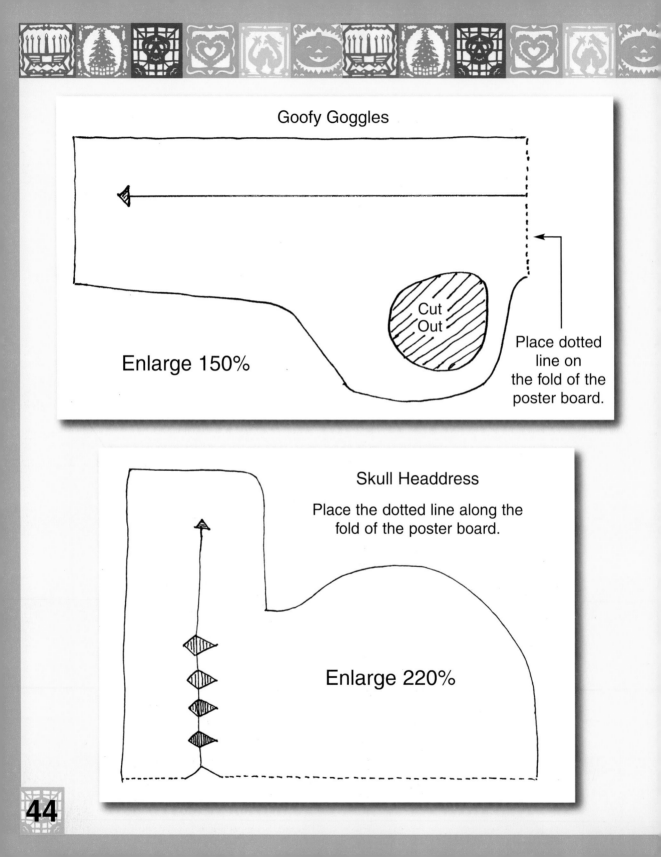

Goofy Goggles

Cut Out

Enlarge 150%

Place dotted line on the fold of the poster board.

Skull Headdress

Place the dotted line along the fold of the poster board.

Enlarge 220%

READ ABOUT

BOOKS

Gillis, Jennifer Blizin. *Halloween*. Chicago, Ill.: Heinemann Library, 2003.

Greene, Carol. *The Story of Halloween*. New York: HarperCollins, 2004.

Haugen, Brenda. *Halloween*. Minneapolis, Minn.: Picture Window Books, 2004.

Sklansky, Amy E. *Skeleton Bones & Goblin Groans: Poems for Halloween*. New York: Henry Holt and Co., 2004.

White, Linda. *Haunting on a Halloween: Frightful Activities for Kids*. Salt Lake City, Utah: Gibbs Smith, 2002.

INTERNET ADDRESSES

Halloween on the Net
<http://www.holidays.net/halloween/>

Halloween
<http://www.enchantedlearning.com/crafts/halloween/>

Visit Randel McGee's Web site at
<http://www.mcgeeproductions.com>

INDEX

A

All Hallow's Even, 4, 5
All Hallows' Mass, 4
All Soul's Day, 5
Americans, 5

B

bat, 11, 20
Bat and Ghost Chains, 20
black cat(s), 24, 28
bonfire(s), 4, 11, 24
broom(s), 24

C

Catholic, 4
Celts, 4, 11
Christianity, 4
costume(s) 5, 24, 34

D

Day of the Dead, 5
decorations, 34
Día de los Muertos, 5
Druids, 4

E

England, 4

F

Flying Bat, 11

G

ghost(s), 15, 20, 31
Goofy Goggles, 34

H

Hallowmas, 5
harvest, 4, 6
Haunted House With Ghosts, 15

I

Ireland, 4

J

jack-o'-lanterns, 5

M

mask(s), 4, 31, 34

P

party, 11, 20
pets, 11, 24, 28

R

Roman(s), 4
ruins, 15, 20

S

saint(s), 4, 5
Samhain, 4
scarecrow, 6
Scarecrow Jumping Jack, 6
Scotland, 4
Sitting Black Cat, 28
skeleton, 31
skull(s), 31
Skull Headdress, 31
soul cakes, 5
spirits, 4, 15, 31
Standing Little Witchie, 24

T

trick-or-treating, 5, 34

U

United States, 5

W

witch(es), 11, 24, 28

ABOUT THE AUTHOR

Randel McGee has been playing with paper and scissors for as long as he can remember. As soon as he was able to get a library card, he would go to the library and find the books that showed paper crafts, check them out, take them home, and try almost every craft in the book. He still checks out books on paper crafts at the library, but he also buys books to add to his own library and researches paper-craft sites on the Internet.

McGee says, "I begin by making copies of simple crafts or designs I see in books. Once I get the idea of how something is made, I begin to make changes to make the designs more personal. After a lot of trial and error, I find ways to do something new and different that is all my own. That's when the fun begins!"

McGee also liked singing and acting from a young age. He graduated college with a degree in children's theater and specialized in puppetry. After college, he taught himself ventriloquism and started performing at libraries and schools with a friendly dragon puppet named Groark. "Randel McGee and Groark" have toured throughout the United States and Asia, sharing their fun shows with young and old alike.

Groark is the star of two award-winning video series for elementary school students on character education: *Getting Along with Groark* and *The Six Pillars of Character.*

In the 1990s, McGee combined his love of making things with paper with his love of telling stories. He tells stories while making pictures cut from

paper to illustrate the tales he tells. The famous author Hans Christian Andersen also made cut-paper pictures when he told stories. McGee portrays Andersen in storytelling performances around the world.

Besides performing and making things, McGee, with the help of his wife, Marsha, likes showing librarians, teachers, fellow artists, and children the fun and educational experiences they can have with paper crafts, storytelling, drama, and puppetry. Randel McGee has belonged to the Guild of American Papercutters, the National Storytelling Network, and the International Ventriloquists' Association. He has been a regional director for the Puppeteers of America, Inc., and past president of UNIMA-USA, an international puppetry organization. He has been active in working with children and scouts in his community and church for many years. He and his wife live in California. They are the parents of five grown children who are all talented artists and performers.